Smaller Hours

smaller hours
KEVIN SHAW

icehouse poetry
an imprint of Goose Lane Editions

Edited by Jeffery Donaldson.
Cover and page design by Julie Scriver.
Cover photo: Life-Of-Pix, Pixabay.com.
Printed in Canada.
10 9 8 7 6 5 4 3 2 1

Library and Archives Canada Cataloguing in Publication

Shaw, Kevin, 1984-, author
    Smaller hours / Kevin Shaw.

Poems.
Issued in print and electronic formats.
ISBN 978-0-86492-999-0 (softcover).--ISBN 978-1-77310-016-6 (EPUB).--
ISBN 978-1-77310-017-3 (MOBI)

I. Title.

PS8637.H3834S63 2017   C811'.6   C2017-902811-1
                                              C2017-902812-X

We acknowledge the generous support of the Government of Canada,
the Canada Council for the Arts, and the Government of New Brunswick.

Goose Lane Editions
500 Beaverbrook Court, Suite 330
Fredericton, New Brunswick
CANADA E3B 5X4
www.gooselane.com

For Ben

Contents

one

two

three

four

one

Bind us in time, O seasons clear, and awe.
— Hart Crane, "Voyages II"

Clocked

One grandfather died before I was born.
One grandfather died six months after.
One left pictures; he resembled Humphrey Bogart.
One left a grey suit and a gold watch.

I learned to tell time, the story of an hour.
I called the position of big and little hands into the other room.
I believed watches had faces to remind us of corpses.
I confused grandfather clocks for the men in their caskets.

Throwback

The infield squared the wayward runner,
framing the missteps of the bullyragged.
I wrenched my body into its windup box—
as seen on television—spit, and readjusted.

Daybreak ushers a thirtysomething pain,
all in penance for being not-thirteen.
Whatever ease in sliding home was leased
the day before, now all limber's lost.

How suburban the urge to steal
that same diamond's glory, when I swore
I'd pinch-hit the future in another city,
not my father's. Yet here I lie

in the same ache of his story, pitching
complaint, an adolescent in extra innings.
The art of losing isn't hard to master?
Try winning.

Leavening

His business was the daily bread,
but Google Maps reveals a luxury
apartment remains instead, a substitute
in the street view of passing time.

A quick rise, from edifice to artefact,
without the mealy truth of hardtack lives
getting left like so many crumbs
in the butter.

A fetishist for the what-if,
I calculate the sack-weight of flour,
the heft of yeast and haul of water,
and thrust kettlebells in shifts

at an industrial dawn. As if
enough reps can build the muscle's memory
of my great-great-grandfather's labour,
with no rest for the lately remembered.

But there's no flex in time's erasure.
What gives? The muscle fibs
in fibrous tears that promise a kind
of closure. Some pasts are not reforged

by pumping iron; I'm only reminded
that he and I share nothing, except
the flesh doming through its repetitions
and sleep atrophied by early morning.

Turing's Time Machine

The ticker tapes have run out,
swallowing ones and zeroes,
while from a perfect and pink aporia
dangles the hell's end of a cigarette
that hisses goodbye, goodbye dear,
goodbye to all that in an ink blot.

I'm crossing old circuits,
secret and serendipitous, but to the naked
eye, merely a site to hack a beery slash
in the navy hours. Supposed utopia
forsaken, the flip side
of a fast one — a fist, or life.

The graffiti curates obscenity
in water closets. The toes tap
epistles in a whore's code.
The living history of silence
is counted in the vibratory instants
between chapel bells.

I'm held under suspension
bridges, or I'm standing aside-eyed
at love, hovering around the urinals,
attuned to the signals: those fleeting gazes gone
to the eye-white narcissi of the neon.
Then, in a flash, I see men safe

in the palm of my hand,
and all our causeways come undone.
In the bar, we text our muscled
apparitions while our want is numbered:
one more for the night, and then we swallow
the zero hour.

Lake Effect

i.

In the cabin, we played the stranger's
records, going down
to the wane of Joni's warped guitar

as waterglass shot across our skin
and later, the Perseids,
August's mirrored nor'easter,

replayed the White Hurricane
of November 1913 in meteors
plucked from a comet's freighted wake.

ii.

I saw through bottle-green and time
and returned to the cabin
a sputtering sailor, whiskey-brined,

the trace of snow in ash on your lip
from the last shared cigarette.
I heard the drafts in the cabin,

the lake's revisions of its past,
and all night, I listened to the lapping
of eight captains' *abandon ship!*

against the docks at Goderich.

iii.

All of our desire in a bloom's day, all a season's
in the spilled salt. I tugged the sunlight
from your beard and licked the horizon.

O weekenders of the heart,
just shuffleboard our bodies
when the ice cream shops have shuttered.

iv.

In November, when the lake casts
its cold-snapped mooring lines
toward the city, we leave each other

the passage of fronts.
Winter only ossifies the ebb:
banks mount up to the second storey,

and will not break.

The Flood of '37

We trace the last of the high-water mark
that salts the city like a ring of sweat.
"& Sons" is all that's left of the old sign
as closing time drains the gay bar. We shake
the end of our invisible ink and look for lifts
in the rain. As all the cabs extinguish their wet
and yellow haloes, downtown's a cliché
of April. We walk up Dundas Street
trading directions instead of names, the vague
pre-dawn disclosure. I want to be alone
if the sun rises, but we can't decide who's closer
and so we're wanderers at the meridian,
on the edge of our small and violet disaster.
We don't want to go to bed but shiver
at the abatement, shouldering this dam
against the other's inevitable disappointment.
I sip the city's drunk history, air hopped
at the brewery, and I imagine my apartment flooded
and all my paperbacks swollen and dispersed,
my pills dissolved and meaningless as grist,
the empty bed a sunken ship. The river has fallen
and I too want to be swept, the era's easy deviant.
But I must believe that instead of drowning
we'd hatch some great escapes, and illicit
trysts would begin again somewhere else,
under a false death's presumed innocence.
We'd overturn the optician's billboard,
use it for a skiff, and staying the course
of press-on stars, we'd drift and drift,
anonymous.

After Hours in Eldon House

The antlers in the papered ossuary
buck time's stilled arrow,
casting the river's forked shadow
against cracked paste and filigree.

There's a pianola in the drawing-room
where the ghosts of redcoats surrender
to a chandelier's bent light, their curio hearts
unbolted by the instrument's common measure,

for we are all old buggers tonight.
Preposterous archaeologists,
we mount the stairs backwards two-by-two
so that our exits entrance the past,

which allows this Orphic spell.
Lifting the velvet rope at the threshold
of the other's pleasure, the red
bedroom opens like a mouth.

My soldier has pulled the maid's
apron from the mannequin in the larder,
and sausaged his hairy thighs inside
splitting the lace and seams,

while I'm lashed in brocade to the four-poster,
gagged with a chapped leather bit, nipples
pinched between two pegs, and tickled pink
with peacock feathers. Trussed up

in a borrowed livery, strapped to the hilt
until I'm dizzy, I come to and find myself
the same again: the invert historian
in a convex looking glass.

Downstairs, I fold up the queen and drop
my green pittance in a Plexiglas box,
and signing the registry alias "Robbie Ross,"
I desert the silent centuries.

Harris Park

The old terraces long eroded, we find other flights
from museum to flood plain, our mired minutes spent
seeding anemones or righting tulips and tiger lilies
according to a century-old design. Inevitably, I fall
headlong into mud, memory, the sugar maples
bleeding sweetly on my palms and the satchel of seeds
torn and flung across the lost gardens below —
the lawns, the willows, the gazebo with its broken
bottles, tampons, condoms, needles: the clear-cut
refusal of privacy. He finds me among morels
and soda cans, tasting of peat, musk, and metal, damp
with sweat and sunk into the green morass
of my own making. *For Julian comes, and he*
what I do to the grass, does to my thoughts and me.

At Lake Horn, ca. 1850

A bent sentinel at the corner, I'm hauled
out to dig for my disorderly conduct
a watering hole so the men might bathe:
me and my unbecoming lip service.

We levelled the hill to dam it,
bound the lake in streets called after
Waterloo, various dukes, or Piccadilly Circus—
our violence by any other name.

I watched their wet asses gleam
for punishment. Later, the water's ruled
unhygienic and Carling's Creek now runs
in the sewers, a man-made lake

drained for the brewers. Later still,
the boys from the bar at the CPR Hotel
walk the rails in the red light of its fail-
safe semaphores, wade into the one-time

shore, their jeans and Calvins stuffed
down around their sneakers. They come
for me in my epaulets and fetish gear,
the boxing sentries shuddering forward.

Yet they're not apart from my detachment's
history here. One or another throws a punch
before dawn. The sun rises to refill
the lake with concrete and crimson.

Victoria Park

The children play on a Sherman tank called the Holy Roller,
sighting ley lines through the park toward St. Peter's door. Sixteen,
I watch the cenotaph's shadow march its sundown parade
while pairs of men in white shirts stop to ask if I've been saved.
I think of Sunlight, stain fighters,

my mother folding boxers with the phone in the crook
of her neck, as she murmurs her observations of me to the doctor.
Have I been tilting at clocks again? St. Peter answers
in the pealing bell at dusk. Our mother Marion,
Our Lady of Sorrows, still worries what befalls some boys

in the river and parks. Meanwhile, city maintenance men
string Christmas lights across the imported forest,
as in 1882 when the park first went electric, and seven thousand
faces turned nickelodeon at the switch, and we other Victorians
bowed beneath the steepled trees and hid.

I meet the boy from school at the southwest cannon,
installed after the Siege of Sevastopol. He leads me round
to a bench in the evergreens (Mom warned me against their shadows)
and as the cathedral sounds the hour, I bloody my tongue
against his braces' barbed wire.

A pair of idlers in a copse, that the police tell to move along,
we surrender. *Flirting with fusiliers, smiling on grenadiers—*
These are the joys of a garrison town. Looking back,
I can't rebuild demolished barracks without playing soldier,
so I run across the melted rink, drowning my image in the water.

To One a Century Hence

Calm and glorious roll the hours here—the whole twenty-four.…
Such a procession of long drawn-out, delicious half-lights nearly
every evening…
　　　—Walt Whitman, *Diary in Canada*, on the grounds of
　　　the London Asylum for the Insane, June and July 1880

Twilight tastes of candied violet, and I carry the coming night
as a tin in my pocket, melting archaic love-me-nots on my tongue.
Ginsberg found you tasting artichokes in California,
yet here you are, conducting the late-arriving stars on Highbury Avenue
in the summer of my hometown. I'm nineteen, or a hundred; the world
dimmed and my room's right angles conspired against me. I walked
kilometres to abandon my body at the side of the road. The doctor
wants me to confess, by way of analysis, the great difficulty of my desire.
What if the morning closed its petals on its own, without some named
　　cruelty?

These are my specimen days; he pins my minutes down, wings of a moth
mounted to his office wall. *Same time Tuesday?* the incremental future calls
and I fold tomorrow, a paper square, into my wallet. You wrote yourself
millennia and bound them in calamus. I'm the one you've reached tonight,
a century hence, walking a lot's labyrinth in the city's permanent
half-light. When you were last here this was countryside, and roses
fired the lawn. Now, yellow lines and an orange sky that betrays our gazing,
though Antares, comrade-in-arms, still rises as it did that evening, 1880.
Now it is you, compact, visible, realizing my poems, seeking me.

two

This is not a home but a collection…
—Daryl Hine, "The Copper Maple"

Occlusion Effect

I kept the memory of my body's discovery,
a stone glassed against adolescence. I survived
an extended dinosaur epoch. Aged ten, eleven
and still I dug in my parent's garden, seeking
fossils and my lost trinkets. I found a cat's-eye
and my old He-Man figurine. That summer,
a guide at the Pinery told me, "All this here
used to be water." As if a single absolution came
and went with the glacier. I treaded time
by taking drags of the undertow. My mother's face
on the shore, there then not there,
until she waved me in with her *Redbook*
reflecting the sun in the glossy pool of its cover.
All this here used to be water. My parents
married in '74 and parted that December. Same
difference. So many bottle caps in the reversing
current. In her jewellery box, my mother kept a rock,
the outline of a shell on its smooth, grey surface.
While I'd dangle her gold clip-ons beside
my buzzed scalp, slowly turn my face
in the mirror, I never pressed the shell in the rock
to my newly bedazzled ears, or listened
for the echo of a bygone ocean. Summer of '96,
summer of dissonance—
                        I kept the memory of the body's
discovery, a stone glassed against adolescence.
Herb Baumeister of Indianapolis, a married
father of three who murdered eleven gay men
and buried them in his backyard at the Fox Hollow
Farm, drove north on the I-75 that July, a river
of ghosted headlights in the rear-view mirror.
Campers found him dead at the Pinery, a self-
inflicted gunshot wound to the head. Years later,

I think of him as I plant rosemary on my balcony.
"That's for remembrance," Ophelia says not long
before drowning. So many summers have lapsed.
I remind myself to look up the meaning of "antediluvian."
Harder still to date my father's going, the instant apogee
of a wave's ebb, or the moment I gained the knowledge
my as-yet-unspoken longing would risk some violence.
Potting reminds me of Baumeister's son, around
my age, who discovered the first skull in the woods
and brought the bones to his mother. She claimed later,
to police and reporters, she suspected nothing.
A childhood news hour replays, but the anchor's
submerged. All this here used to be water.

Allium cepa

In biology, the first specimen was an onion's skin, perhaps to acquaint us

with dailiness. I set the focus of the scope and sluiced

blue against the glass — the cells like swelled seigneurial plots

banking iodine rivers, or the stretch-marked topography

of my father's belly, which he once claimed as scars from a bear.

I suppose the lesson remains that things are like other things

though there's always a stranger word for what's familiar —

cataphyll for the onion bulb's epidermal interiors —

and the reminder that etymologies are not roots, but flowers.

Produce derives from a Latin verb meaning to lengthen,

to lead, or to yield. I remember *celeriter* means quickly

because my Latin teacher once observed the word resembles *celery*,

a vegetable he ate with haste because it was bland.

Onion skins flake to my kitchen floor most evenings, or

cling to the sides of the reusable shopping bag, missives from old

marketing. In the typing pool, onionskin paper once lay over carbon

to produce memoranda in duplicate. My great-uncle's letters

arrived on onionskin, too, though his memory failed

even its reproductions: in the end, he thought he was twelve years old
   again,

and we neither of us remembered the rules of cricket, though he'd say

it was just like baseball. Things are like other things even when they're
   not.

Like how his daughter who spoke in tongues drafted his last letters

until he didn't know her, so many Our Fathers sung otherwise.

We say there are no words in grief: food

fills our mouths at a funeral. But isn't cooking always a translation?

To weep discreetly: mince words and slice the onions.

Peppermint

An invasive species, lust.
Its roots less stubborn than
gluttonous: the seedy tourist
writhing under all-inclusive sun,
drunk on rain. *Best to keep*
its roots contained,
we read too late.

Dig its rhizomes,
pull the arterial knot,
and you've got
a summer's mangled valentine,
while six feet away, three plants fall:
you never know who hurts
in the other marriage.

That night, we ate the green
hearts with jagged edges
muddled in boozy juleps,
and soused our reserve.
The next day, making tea
from the leaves,
we sipped in a sprung silence.

That old elixir of excess
and emperors, used to loosen
belches before orgies,
was drunk not in remorse
by immoderate Romans,
but to make room for more
between the courses.

Open

Afterward, I stumbled home
and the flashing stoplight tried to bloom

in the fog. I thought of my mouth.
He and I up half the night, drunk,

the taste of a stranger's honeyed stigma
fresh as bee spit on my tongue and lip.

Gather ye rosebuds while ye may.
Don't I gather buds, and their baskets too?

The Chili

It hung, a long face barely hitched
to the nervous neck of stem, pathetic
mane of yellowed leaves dropping
before the first dried thistles
could catch in the eaves. All summer

I watched the small white flowers
bloom and wilt, leaving green stubs
unfulfilled. The solitary chili refused
to redden or die, sequestered the heat
of the sun inside, a heft of light

that would surely snap the plant in half.
But I hesitated to harvest this last hope,
as if the blight could be beaten still,
and if the pepper held on, we would, too,
or our plot was just another empty bed.

"Maybe it's a metaphor," he said,
half-joking, though one early morning
I cut the stem and threw down
that damn chili dead. I later told him
it was a squirrel that felled it.

Assembly

The Allen keys I kept for the prefab apocalypse
would fill the museum of late modern love.
I confused a sublet for sublimation
until the couch didn't fit the doorframe
and the cupboards betrayed the scent
of what they once held. So I spent the night
unboxing headless men from their squares
on the grid instead of my belongings.
Because the heart burns and people go on
eating hot dogs, I window shopped domesticity
in the showroom, wondering why we didn't
have designs on each other anymore.
Perhaps because the ice cubes in the shape of fish
survived us. Perhaps because our houseguests
fingered the potted cypress and had to ask,
"Is this real?" And even after all these years
the instructions for putting things together
remain only gestural, like reading a shoulder.

Sailor, Detroit Riverfront

He strokes the wet sidewalk with legs as long as oars.
We're walking one behind the other but I'm caught
in the wake of him. *What letter stroke*
would walking be? An "I" stroke, obviously.
I bob beyond him, portly as a life preserver
flung out to sea, to see his legs as long as oars.

My steps hail, flat feet plunked in deepening puddles,
but his steps elide, each foot the other, and his legs long,
as oars do, for the water. He wears an Old Navy sweater:
horizontal grey and royal blue, hint of undershirt
at the hem, seafoam rising above the bilge
and those legs as long as oars.

George Eliot

That bed not big enough for the both of us,
though called, of course, a twin, where we two

larger men unmade its sheets and comforter
to make ourselves instead. There we lay

head to toe, pit to crown, or sack to chin,
bending the bounds of symmetry, and then

the bed. Our hearts must be heavy, you said,
still giddy with beer and novelty, when

we decided to observe the Hays code, and keep
one foot on the floor. I leveraged against

Middlemarch, abandoned for the bar,

as I'd left it, unread, twice before.
That was no time to think of England, but

I wondered about Casaubon, and if
we'd finish our works, and by our own hand.

In that sinking bed, were we both Jonah
and Leviathan? And would we finish anything—

books, cigarettes, each other? That bed,
our bodies, the novel—take it all

together—we could spend a century reading
and never come to the other's ending.

Epistle

Remember that winter we lived together, and bought
the same wool coat? Mine was the larger,

so when I wore yours by mistake, you tugged
at my shoulder, though you were upstairs asleep.

Your collar smelled like October, smelled like
a neck of woods in the sun. Though you moved on

and out, the coat hangs in my closet still, your pockets full
of gum wrappers, an Air Miles card. Sometimes,

I think of that Mallory who might've summited
Everest in '24, undiscovered there for seventy-five years,

and the packet of letters the climbers recovered
from a body cold-fired to porcelain. To when,

not whom, were the letters delivered?

What Not to Wear

Each night about this time he puts on sadness like a garment
and goes on writing.
—Anne Carson, "Short Talk on Ovid"

As the exiled dress without mirrors,
he exchanged a tunic for the elegiac couplet.

Word-weary, I would tattoo a wilted
pansy on my bicep,

wear sweatpants in translation
from a dead language. To say as much

is silence. I unfold anxiety in triplicate,
a screen in some well-appointed

corner. The dropped ball of Y-front briefs,
a questioning desire.

Lycra is optimism. Oxford, ire.
Sleeveless tees shirk my heart and letters.

A book on closet design suggests
I ask the pairs of socks and trousers:

do you bring me joy?
Discard whatever vestments

make me cry. So, goodbye forever
size 32 blue denim jeans and the ex's

leather. I box my well-worn sentiment
for the Goodwill and deliver it,

a prodigal from the laundromat
disguised by toque and sunglasses.

Did Ovid at Pontus mount such obvious
productions of himself, or simply shoulder

the sad and foregone outfit, knowing
a makeover is not a metamorphosis?

three

Musicians wrestle everywhere—
—Emily Dickinson, "#157/F229"

Harmonica

Such intimacy,
to make music making a kiss,

and there's pleasure here, too,
in the translation

of breath to a chord
forged with the tongue.

These bronze-shimmied
breezes…as if I could,

as if I could make meadow music
like the invisible player of long grasses.

But what is an open C, if not hope?
First attempt at bending the note

seems an impossible sleight of lung
pitched imperfectly, a tumbling

of apocryphal sound I'd rather keep
between instrument and closed palm,

but the metal must sing
the breath's undulation —

my body pushes and the harp pulls.
Afterward, mouth bruised with vibration,

my tongue tastes a blue note
buzzing on the edge of my lip.

Mixtape

That year of unreliable pitch,
I magnetized my junior high
fidelities: set ten songs to say more
for the record than passing notes.
We long-played every lunch,
sitting earbud-to-bud on bleachers
clouded with our body sprays
and odour: that was the end
of my youth, or Side A.
Because he knew then, and voiced
in a newly minor key, how
these singles somehow leaked
my different frequency, or timbre.
Proving even the greatest hits
poor cover, he left me to the tune
of Cyndi Lauper's "True Colors."

Expired Trojan

Like this could mean so much more
than an old want squared
away in a shoeboxed decade
unfolding its past geometries.

How I foiled my first hopes.
Pressed a horizontal prayer
between wallet's pleathered sides
and was still found bent.

Next, a perforated fear.
Anxious soldier snuck in by night
to breach *le village*, or
its sweaty dancers at the perimeter.

For the man who said,
so retro, "Got a rubber?"
yes, you spun me right round.
Pocketed preserver

kept by a whimsy
in the belowground
of my smaller hours,
a whimsy also expired.

Song

We karaoke the dead in Molly Bloom's
Irish Pub—Janis Joplin, Freddie Mercury—
and then the forgotten hits of the noughts
and nineties, the songs we danced to
in our previous youths, for we have shaved
our North Faces and are youths anew,
living again in our parents' basements.

Best night ever proclaimed by parting
friends and lovers. I'm left alone at 3 a.m.
to eat chips and shawarma with my head-
phones on, Gladys Knight's "Midnight
Train to Georgia" laying the tracks one
over another, as I hum the railroad home
or eastward until the battery's dead.

Now, I hear men nearby in patterns
of familiar sound and action: a dry night's
wet end to abstention, or the sought echo
found amid the side-rail bushes—hushed
voices, slapping flesh, and a disembodied
strain lacking melody or lyric. Impossible
to remember, recount, or play it.

Audition

The waiting room is a wing
of a strange ballet, as if you're auditioning
for a role in your sexual history,
though you are not yourself today.

Please take a number.
Have a seat and we'll call your number
then you'll tell the nurse the number
of partners that you've had, and the number

of times and kinds of unprotected sex
you've enjoyed in the past number of months.
Then the nurse at the station will take your urine
and you'll pray your Saturday nights don't catch.

This evening, you're Nijinsky
of the Ballets Russes, counting the measure
of your night moves, while the doctor
charts the lines of your body.

No judgment, of course, except of your veins
which the doctor says are deep,
narrow, and difficult to see,
unlike the spot you've been sweating, which,

with your jeans around your knees,
she says is definitely not HPV,
herpes, or molluscum contagiosum (a magic spell?)
but just some benign accident of cells.

Then you're back with the waiting
in *La danse des regards évités*,
and as you jeté toward the exit, a nurse shouts:
callbacks are in seven days.

Epithalamium

"This would have to happen right before [Eric and Jack's]
wedding. The reception was going to be held at the Stonewall,
too," Nan said, tossing her ashen-tinted hair over her shoulder.
—Jerry Lisker, "Homo Nest Raided, Queen Bees Are
Stinging Mad," *New York Daily News*, July 6, 1969

Names of no registry, the confetti
in pennies and beer,

as the siren seduces
New York's finest

queens toward a fierce dawn.
Flora of pepper spray,

first dance in fisticuffs.
The names of no registry, the confetti

in cinders—
cash registers battered—

while streamers
of lighter fluid

arc through windows once dark.
A catcall officiates

the names of no registry. The confetti
of stars, unseen

from alleyways.
A kick line chants

fag power! take over!
and street kids swish

aisles in anger,
in the name of no registry. The confetti

of cigarettes
spills ash on foreheads,

while wigs tossed as bouquets
explode on Impalas.

Witnesses reported,
and we don't remember,

the names of no registry, the confetti
of glass.

Guglielmo Marconi Sends My Regrets

Marconi's law — that the extent of a transmission
is the square of the antenna's height —

does not apply to the afterlife, and yet
I spent those final minutes counting silences.

History embarrasses. Heroes disappoint.
Grandsons disavow inheritance, birthright.

I won't be married at the Marconi Club,
Nonna. I won't take a wife.

The man with whom I lived was not
my roommate.

The Jordan almonds remain in tulle,
pastel blue, preserved, inedible. Imagine

Lombardo still plays New Year's Eve,
live remote from the bar at the Roosevelt.

Should auld acquaintance be forgot,
and never brought to mind?

My voice telegraphs through time
as if by wireless. I confess, Nonna, I confess —

Emile Berliner on Desert Island Discs

That year we drank, castaways from the wreck
of our twenties, carrying long-distance, polyamorous
valises from the decade we couldn't leave.

You took an alias or three. Presented yourself
at dive bars and house parties, the twentieth-century
raconteur or imp, the last of all the straight boys

I fell in love with a moment. Emile, the man who pressed
the first disc record in lampblack and varnish, ca. 1887.
Your last-call voicemails, with an inventor's fervour,

willed me from my bed to bar or apartment, to drink
whiskey and smoke cigarettes as we traded notes
for the examination, distilling James into Jameson's.

Never mind — another round — while you played me
the Beach Boys' *Pet Sounds* on the turntable
in your attic. We traded frankly — O'Hara, gossip —

and shouted Donne at the empty street: *No man
is an island!* Entirely single and pretentious;
my relationship had ended. Moored between

Victorian bachelors, we slept together in that bed
fit for a queen, perhaps more nights than I really needed.
Though I wanted to rest in the endless pop and hiss

of the last record's afterward, I woke before you,
pulled on my jeans and boots, and left
by the fire escape, without ever lifting the needle.

Alexander Graham Bell

How would we have spent our quarter
hours, had we hated each other?
Answering the body's call
requires such risk in the reception.

I'm the kind of guy who says
he's not the kind of guy who meets
a man he barely knows at the GO
station, yet there we were

making the connection. OKCupid
put our odds at three-to-one.
You said let's try being
an algorithmic exception, and relayed

that day to evening. In 1876,
Bell patented the voice's transmission
by "electrical undulations," mimicking
the vibration of air carrying the word.

And weren't we yet another twisted pair,
our coppers taut and stripped
bare, encoding the very crosstalk
we were meant to disavow, not enamour?

But you held the line, tongued
post-to-post along my spine, follicles
alighting as a colony of gulls takes flight
only to resettle that same cable.

I slept as sound as a switchboard
now, in your loft converted from the old
Bell tower. Strange how the half-risen walls
never met their ceilings, exposing

their vents and wires. I went naked
from bed to shower, caught in static
the trace of a former operator,
and through the glass watched you shave

in the fogged mirror. What's the difference
between intimacy and exposure
when the private line goes down? I heard
your neighbour's phone ring, unanswered.

Thomas Edison

As his cylinder unrolls a second,
I set my lips against the diaphragm,
blow an opening bar's waveform, and
with tongue for a needle in hill and dale,
graph the veins of his Blue Amberol.

To play it back, he slides it over, winds
the spring of his reproducer, and sets
a diamond stylus into the familiar groove.
I'm born again in music: a whole note
sustained, horn-blasted.

four

and the blood in my pants mounts to the stars
as I ponder the silver square
— Frank O'Hara, "In the Movies"

Coming Attractions '98/'99

Gods and Monsters

At fifteen, I incarnated
Frankenstein's monster,
sought a father's pardon
and gelled my Caesar.

I'd resurrected James Whale
at the Blockbuster Video;
he was alive and well
and living in suburban Ontario.

I stalked the school halls
a second-string punter.
Whale framed my angles;
I wanted his gardener

(that Brendan Fraser....)
Each night, I made a man
by rewinding parts, desire
binding him to my hand.

The Mummy

We drank milkshakes before the movie;
a white moustache smeared my lip.
Rick tagged the guy a *Dairy Queen*
faggot. I downed my guilt in sips.

A white moustache smeared my lip
some nights with Rick; he never called me
faggot. I downed his guilt in sips.
I swallowed salt for the memory.

Jell All

about the time I sailed Sal Mineo's eye
guided by an overturned bowl of stars
with a pomaded sun rising in the reflection
of James Dean's scalloped forehead
capped in perfect crescents of concern
and I coasted my sixteenth summer there
in a repertory's run of *Rebel without a Cause*
sipping orangeade from Sal's right clavicle
through a very long striped straw
as I played my favourite game
Hot or Not in the magazines a cool confessor
all the while Sal playing as he lies
dead in James Dean's arms and I paparazzo
hiding in the iris pool turning tabloid history
to borrow a pulped martyrdom in an inky theatre
where Sal always falls in love or sin the subject
of a million boys' disconnected gazes (even now
looking? looking? yet never held there)
as I was buoyed the time I sailed Sal's eye
or first saw *The New Adam* all senses hung
on the wall of thigh and the museum-goers
haloed by areolae forty feet of painted flesh
three walls and still Stevenson can't fit him all in
and hides Sal's face as Adam covers his eyes
unlearning shame lapsed grace lost fame

After Jack Chambers's
401 Towards London No. 1

I've made a triptych of my leaving town.
The trouble remains, you can go home
again and again and again…

In Montreal, I waited for him at arrivals
carrying a baker's dozen day-old bagels
I swore to myself I'd never versify.

He said, "Now you wear your scarf
on the outside," before we boarded
the Metro in the wrong direction.

After I deplaned in Saskatoon, years later,
I received a pocket-dialed message:
his footsteps as he left departures in the snow.

That night, I slept under *The Last Supper*
as painted by the octogenarian owner
of a Prince Albert B & B — how do we

frame the minutes just before our going?
Another September, another leaving —
London for Windsor — I mistook the east-

bound ramp for west. The slanted city
hung in the rear-view's movable past —
objects appearing closer than reality.

Voicemail

As if you could unwrap my breath in bubble wrap, or find
the teeth enunciating in the metal mailboxes, or pay
cash-on-demand for the shape of my lips kissing a coy vowel

into speech. My weary timbre, affixed to the corner of this call—
the longing posts between provinces. Can I get a feeling
from here to there, expressed overnight and undeclared?

Accept these charges: all of my complaints crowding in against
your ear in the morning, because I forgot the time difference
again, or pretended to, because I wanted to race the sunlight

to your bed, because it always gets to you before I do.
I just called to say I need you. Do you still need me too?
Remember me, like you remember the milk.

Layover

The terminal made us both familiar,
nationals of nowhere, equally suspect.
We drank together in the airport bar
pitching pints, delimiting our prospects
at twenty-five. Joe from Ireland
right pissed and ready for takeoff. He said
he crossed an ocean to see his girl in
Montreal and his queer mate had yet to bed
a man and wasn't that sad and love strange?
We turned over our lives just as tabloid
pages thumbed before departure, changed
to starkness of newsprint, our lives void
of private matters. Then, we left each other
as one leaves behind that local paper.

Only Connect

We're night-poor in the city, robbed of our diamond
similes. The reflection of the billboard in the window
casts a fifty-foot GoodLife torso down Queen West,
as the man throws wool shadows against the closet,
watch and wedding band unhanded to the desk.

Let us be wilful nobodies at the hourly palace.
Let the double-bleached sheets erase all traces
of previous guests. Let the happy-hour specials
at the hotel bar (half-off domestic pitchers)
make the blazered in business class grin, like

boarding-school teens getting away with something.
Only connect—even if the wi-fi's glitchy, and we
rebuff Church Street's 24-hour turndown service
for some anonymity… By the raw light of dawn,
a stranger, I can be any man, or any man's aubade.

Discretion

send pics with personal
ads are now known as Casual
encounters in the corner of the touch
screenings held at the clinic available
MWM seeking NSA fun with
masculine men a plus and negative
as of March 1st drug and disease free-
loaders need not apply
stats available upon request
that you be str8-acting too
much cologne is a turn
often available on weeknights after
work out 6 days a
weak sissies need not
a requirement but a plus-
size queens step to the back
doors open at six bring your own
condoms are an absolute
musclebear seeking same for
none of the gay stuff just
time next week available for
companionship and possibly more
leather the better cuz I love me some
uncut guys are OK
to contact this user directly press
200 pounds on the bench 150
max. since I don't do fat
ass is high and willing to please
be discreet

Oscar Wilde on Grindr

What is it to be adored, but suffering
boredom in the face of another's want?

Reel

They remain in silent fictions, flickers
in the zoetrope of the landscape,
expectant spectators, their hands hinged
on the lapsing flash of daybreak.

It may be the fleeting affinity
of hurtling steel that calls up
our kindnesses to the outside world —
but don't get me wrong:

I won't speak with my seatmate, either.
Though I want the old man on a folding chair,
dozing auteur of the Brockville tracks,
to know he's known to the blur.

The most I'll know of the woman
from somewhere beyond Gananoque
is the instant between wind-whipped linens
she stands with a hug of underpants in her arms.

At least we give each other a story of the day.
A man across the aisle
chins up and snaps a selfie.
We make spectacles of our going away.

Perhaps those who wave at passing trains
are the ones who shoot us for the screen test.
Everyone is more or less a remake
of Eva Marie Saint in *North by Northwest*.

In the reels between the major cities
we exchange excitement for ennui
with the ones who wave from the crossing
in the brief aperture of our leaving.

Retrospect: After Margaret Watkins

i.

Our going seems inevitable. Sweat wells
in the small and cobalt of his shirt
as we shunt picture to picture through the museum
framing innuendo, weak arrows seeking consent.

That is definitely a phallic symbol, he says.

I want to see through fever in a sepia print,
or a maelstrom in the developing pool
where I'll rise to my drowned occasion,
but viewing the Thames through tinted windows
I'm but a cyanotype in translation. We enter
late afternoon where the river forks.

ii.

Tracking Dundas to Richmond Row heading north,
I watch the people she shot — from Moscow
to New York — looking in shop windows.

I use him in the same way, to invert myself
and see through to the end of want.

iii.

The Dominion leans its Deco shadows
against St. Paul's Gothic tower.

In her photograph, a man's shoes and trousers
swing from iron scaffolding above the frame.

iv.

In my yellow rooms, the golden hour turns
bilious. I practice my twentieth-century poses
while he undresses. The emptied tube sock,
the end of a blue movie.

Crowdsourcing

The Earth tilts its axis, a drunk uncle
spilling oceans from his gimlet, or

a red giant consumes the planet
as a morning-after Alka-Seltzer tablet:

either way, we should've left the party
before the eschatologist

half-raised our indeterminacies. Turns out,
ardour and the sun dim a little more each day.

Given a terminal erection, I'd still ask
is this love or the apocalypse, doubting

Thomases, Dereks, Jims, and Kenneths.
Now, I wish I'd neither sought nor read

Wikipedia's "List of Dates Predicted
for the End of the Earth"

waiting for you to brush your teeth
and come to bed. Because the superbugs

will have adapted and the poles swelter or
droughts will starve us if an asteroid doesn't

befall us sooner, we might as well edit
these end times together.

We'll stop all the clocks and recant
the Top 40 tracts of planetary collapse

in an instant. Studies show Wikipedia's vandals
stand corrected within eleven seconds.

We'll count down from ten to one
and be immortal for the moment.

NOTES

"Throwback" quotes Elizabeth Bishop's "One Art."

The italicized lines in "Harris Park" are adapted from Andrew Marvell's "The Mower's Song."

"Victoria Park" borrows lines from an unknown London, ON, poet, possibly a soldier, ca. 1840, as quoted in Orlo Miller's *London 200: An Illustrated History*.

The final line of "To One a Century Hence" is from Walt Whitman's *Leaves of Grass*.

"Open" quotes Robert Herrick's "To the Virgins, to Make Much of Time."

In "Guglielmo Marconi Sends My Regrets," the italicized lines quote Robert Burns's "Auld Lang Syne."

ACKNOWLEDGEMENTS

Earlier versions of some poems first appeared in the following journals, sometimes under different titles. I'm grateful to the editors of each.

Arc Poetry Magazine: "Turing's Time Machine"
Contemporary Verse 2: "Tell All"
Fiddlehead: "Expired Trojan," "Alexander Graham Bell," and "Reel"
Grain: "Leavening," "Throwback," and "Audition"
Malahat Review: "Harmonica"
Plenitude: "Discretion"
PRISM international: "The Flood of '37"

I want to thank everyone at icehouse poetry and Goose Lane, especially Ross Leckie for his enthusiasm and encouragement. Thank you to Jeffery Donaldson for his generous and careful attention to these poems.

Thank you to Madeline Bassnett, Tom Cull, David Huebert, Blair Trewartha, and Andy Verboom for being the best first readers.

Thank you to the Department of English at Western, and especially to Manina Jones for her encouragement over the years.

To my friends Donnie Calabrese, Emily Kring, Riley McDonald, and Meghan O'Hara: thank you for reading and for all the retro nights.

Thank you to my family and friends, especially Jordan Murray, for their understanding.

Finally, with love and thanks to Ben Jaremko.

Photo by Ben Jaremko

Kevin Shaw was born and raised in London, Ontario. His poems have appeared in the *Malahat Review*, the *Gay & Lesbian Review*, *Contemporary Verse 2*, *Grain*, and the *Fiddlehead*. He received the Arc Poetry Magazine Poem of the Year award and the Grand Prize in the PRISM international Poetry Contest. He recently completed his PhD in English at the University of Western Ontario.